MW01148231

Stephen Curry

The Inspirational Story of One of the Greatest

Basketball Players of All Time!

By Patrick Thompson

Table of Contents

INTRODUCTION

One of today's most sought-after NBA superstars was once a young boy who was perceived as weak. Despite this humble beginning, he has managed to rise from his simple life in North Carolina into becoming one of the sharpest shooters in the history of the NBA.

Stephen Curry's journey to becoming one of NBA's legends has been tough and rocky. He might be the son of another NBA veteran, but his journey towards his dreams was not smooth-sailing. He also had his fair share of rejections and doubts – both from himself and others.

However, years of diligent practice helped him perfect his dazzling and surprising moves on the court. It allowed him to step up and lead his team, the Golden State Warriors, to numerous wins.

This book will give you

a peek into Stephen Curry's personal life so you can get to know the superstar better. Beyond the basketball accolades, the Baby-faced Assasin is a loving husband and father. He also has his own stories of fear, trials, and touching moments. After all, Stephen Curry has remained a human.

CHAPTER 1
WHO IS STEPHEN CURRY?

THE GOLDEN BOY OF BASKETBALL

Blessed with incredible abilities to make a smooth-sailing shot from any distance, amazing hand-eye coordination, intelligent mastery of the game, and marvelous three-point prowess, Stephen Curry has become a supernova, changing the face of the NBA.

The 6-foot-3-inche Baby-faced Assassin obviously lacks physical boldness and size. However, do not be fooled by his soft aura of charm; Stephen Curry can transform into a big dog when fighting a hardcourt battle. He can strike fear through his jaw-dropping moves, demoralizing his opponent's defense.

Yet his merciless presence on the court is simply about the pursuit of excellence and respect. He plays not to embarrass his opponents but simply to win – whether *he* becomes the top scorer or not. He makes sure that the conquest benefits his team and not himself. Perhaps this is the reason why Stephen Curry has become one of the most positive stars in the NBA.

In less than a decade, Stephen has managed to win the hearts of many people along with a long list of accolades. The 30-year-old charmer is a two-time MVP and has three Championship Awards under his belt. In 2016, he made history by being the first player in the NBA to get a unanimous vote for the MVP Award – and he was the first Golden State Warrior to get the MVP Award in 55 years.

Alongside players like Magic Johnson, Michael Jordan, and LeBron James, Curry holds the record of being the 11th player (and third point guard) to win a back- to-back MVP trophy.

Curry's offensive prowess and shooting accuracy have redrawn the map of the point guard landscape. Even though the NBA is dominated by highly-skilled point guards, Curry was able to stand out and make his mark through elegant showmanship. He never seems to run out of moves that keep his opponents guessing.

As a captain of the team, Stephen Curry allows his teammates to thrive off of his selflessness. He often uses his gravitational pull to attract the defense towards him and make room for his brothers.

Despite being known for their high expectations, NBA fans and critics are surprisingly pleased by Curry's brilliant ball-passing skills and scoring abilities.

With a whooping average of 23 points per game, there is no doubt that Curry was able to redeem himself from all the doubt thrown at him during his pre-NBA career. In 2015, the year the Golden

State bagged its first championship in 40 years, Curry held the torch and led the team to a historical 26-1 record. It is clear that Curry has become the Warriors' winning ace.

In a game against the Minnesota Timberwolves in January 2018, Curry showed off his strong offense. Blocked by two defenders, Curry made a quick dribble that split the obstacles. The point guard hero quickly made a pullup and a mid-range jump shot. That moment was marked in history as when Curry achieved a career-high of 14,000 points.

With all the accolades, Curry never fails to keep his feet flat on the ground. With a driven and humble character, Curry says that there is still much more he hopes to achieve. He believes that his milestones are still small compared to that of other NBA players and legends like LeBron James. This kind of mindset, thinking that there are still others who are far better than him, is one of the things that keeps the superstar grounded.

DARLING OF THE CROWD

Alongside Stephen Curry's marvelous moves and sharp-shooting skills is a child-like aura that the media describes as crazy likable. Sports enthusiasts and analysts say that Steph is one of, if not the most, celebrated NBA superstars in the world of social media.

Stephen Curry has 21.7 million followers on Instagram, 12.7 million on Twitter, and 8.2 million on Facebook. Fans are raving about Curry's posts which are mostly about his family, particularly about his love for his wife. Instagram followers, being mostly females, find his posts adorable and inspiring.

"He is the first Twitter star of the NBA," reporter Chris Connelly says about Curry. After each game, clips of Curry's moves and plays make the rounds on social media. He goes viral more than any other NBA player does.

In fact, a recent analysis by a branding company revealed that Stephen Curry is the public's top choice for an NBA player in terms of trust ratings, influence, appeal and aspiration.

In terms of aspiration, the category which reflects how relatable a celebrity is, Stephen is just one rank behind Warren Buffet.

According to *Forbes*, Stephen's No. 30 jersey was the second top-selling item in the NBA's 2015 season.

Basketball analysts say that Curry is different from most celebrated NBA ballers, who often associate influence with money and fame. He is perceived as an NBA hero with strong faith and good family values. Despite the accolades, Stephen has remained human. This kind of humility allows the public to see him as someone akin to their neighbor, the person who delivers their mail, or the friendly waiter at a restaurant. He has a magical aura that inspires people to excel yet still appears humble enough to be seen as someone relatable.

Steph credits his endearing character to his lack of dominating physical attributes. "I am just like them. I am obviously not the biggest and I also cannot jump the highest. I am even not the strongest. So, when people see me, they see me just as a normal person," Steph says.

On the court, Steph is often seen laughing and smiling in the middle of a game. Steph's connection with the fans and public is strenghtened by his good demeanor. Growing up tagging along with his dad to almost every practice, Steph saw how connection can affect fans and people. He saw how a simple smile from a player can make anyone's day.

The "Crowd Favorite" title was obvious during the Warriors' Championship parade in June 2018. In front of the hundreds of cheerful fans wanting to catch even a glimpse of the champions, Curry escaped from his security team and ran into the crowd. He ran around the barricades to greet and shake hands with as many fans as he could. Caught by surprise, the security team chased after him but failed to stop Curry from doing his usual thing – making fans and people happy.

The media, being known as one of the toughest critics of NBA players and the NBA itself, find it hard to look for grey areas about Stephen Curry. There are anecdotes from the press sharing how Stephen is humanly humble. Despite the tight schedules, he accepts as many requests as he can – for interviews, photo opportunities, and video greetings. Another thing the press loves about Stephen is that his mastery goes beyond the game. He can talk about many other things and does not mind sharing his thoughts. According to the media, Stephen breathes genuine selflessness. They never get quotations from Steph saying that he is the alpha male of the team or he needs to take all the credit. He admits to what goes wrong on the court. He humbly owns up to his mistakes and shares his plans to make them right. The press always sees him as someone who lacks drama and is full of fun.

Indeed, "genuine" is the perfect word to describe Stephen Curry. People from different walks of life can all relate to him.

Curry sees himself as someone who blends into the crowd. He knows his own weaknesses yet never feels intimidated. He knows he can't make shots akin to his teammates' big moves. This, he believes, is one of the reasons why he fits in. He sees himself as someone just like anybody else.

THE PATRON SAINT OF UNDERDOGS

Phrases like "The Chosen One" can never be tagged with Stephen Curry's name, when talking about his pre-NBA career. Curry had to work hard – doubly hard, in fact – at every point of his career to create the legacy he has today.

Some may think that being born to well-known athletic parents was the ace that helped Stephen make it big. However, even his father's long stint in the NBA still did not make basketball a walk in the park for Stephen. Coaches and university programs used to see nothing in him but his puny body. He was an underdog; shuffled behind the players who seemed to have more potential.

According to his father, Stephen was always the smallest player on a team. In high school, one of the biggest challenges he faced was to play a good game despite not being the most athletically gifted boy.

Curry was often mistaken for a younger player

and his teammates and opponents looked at him as just another kid on the court.

Stephen was born into a wealthy family. Still, not everything was handed to him on a silver platter, especially in terms of his basketball career.

Before Stephen Curry became the sought-after player he is today, no coaches were knocking on his door. His "weak" appearance prevented him from being a highly recruited prospect for college teams.

Every player who dreams of entering the most prestigious basketball league in the world knows the importance of a college offer. A collegiate powerhouse can be a stepping-stone into entering the NBA. However, Stephen Curry had none of it. With his skinny frame and 165-pound mass, Steph was never seen by college scouts as having much strength.

Yet he refused to feel defeated and used his games with a minor college team to work his way up. The ignored player was able to prove himself to all the doubters.

People began to see big skills and a big future growing from the body they considered small. Stephen Curry had a lot of beautiful contradictions in his body. He was a late bloomer whose skill grew faster than his body.

Despite the lack of interest from powerhouse teams, the people who took time to watch Curry's games and moves saw something different as he grew into MVP-caliber. The people who took a chance with him knew that despite the lack of size and build, Curry had everything else.

Stephen Curry fought against all odds to get to where he is today – a huge reminder for every aspirant to continue growing despite challenges.

CHAPTER 2
CHILDHOOD YEARS

IT RUNS IN THE BLOOD

Sports could be considered the universe of the Curry Family. Their world revolves around athletics. Stephen's mother, Sonya, used to play basketball and volleyball for Radford High School. She had a colorful athletics career: winning championships and breaking records. She had the sixth "Most Aces Recorded in a Single Season," when she played for Virginia Tech.

Later on, Sonya would meet an equally athletic man named Wardell. Since Wardell was also a basketball player from Virginia Tech, he was invited to watch one of Sonya's games. He instantly fell in love with her and asked her out on a date right after the game.

In 1988, Sonya and Dell got married, beginning the genealogy of a celebrated sports family.

Dell Curry is imprinted in the history of sports as a long-time sharpshooter and 16-year NBA veteran. He also holds the record of highest total points (9,839) and total three-pointers (929) for the Charlotte Hornets.

He was playing for the Cleveland Cavaliers when his future-superstar son, Wardell Stephen Curry II, was born on March 14, 1988 in Ohio. Stephen, or Steph, was introduced to basketball in his infancy. There was a miniature basketball hoop attached to his crib, which kept him entertained all day.

The family moved to North Carolina when Dell signed on with the Charlotte Hornets. This is where Stephen spent most of his childhood.

Basketball was a huge part of Stephen's childhood routine. Oftentimes, Dell would take his son to his NBA practices. "I used to play around the gym and imitate his shots simply because he was my father," Steph says.

The young Stephen inherited his parents' love for sports. He tried playing not just basketball but also baseball, football, and soccer. Among these, Stephen seemed to have excelled best in baseball until he fell in love with golf at 6 years old, which he played with his father. Later on, he decided to give up baseball and golf because he felt that basketball occupied the biggest space in his heart.

As a family, the Currys would often gather around and play sports – both indoor and outdoor. During their play times, Dell would often talk about the gospel of sports.

Sonya and Dell gave their full support to Stephen and his siblings without pushing their own agendas. They did not impose what kind of sports their children would to play. They allowed them to pick for themselves.

Growing up in the athletics world themselves, Sonya and Dell believe that being a good sportsman is a process, one that begins by letting the child love what he does. This is why Stephen's learning and working came so easily as he achieved new levels, step by step.

Stephen's two younger siblings, Seth and Sydel, were also bestowed with marvelous athletics genes. Seth is currently playing in the NBA as well, making points for the Dallas Mavericks. The youngest of the three, Sydel, followed in her mother's footsteps as a volleyball player for Elon University.

THE SUMMER OF TEARS

Stephen's grandfather, Wardell "Jack" Curry, was one of the first people to introduce Dell to basketball. One summer day, the Curry patriarch put up a basketball ring in their backyard. It was the only way he could think of to keep Dell away from the feminine things scattered around their house. Dell was the only boy in a brood of five.

The hoop stood on an old wooden pole. It had an unforgiving rim made of thick steel. The rim was designed so that only a sharp, well-calibrated shot to the middle of the ring would pass through. Above was a street lamp that illuminated the hoop at night. The self-made basketball ring was positioned near a muddy area. The only way to keep the ball from getting muddy was to make sure that it got perfectly shot into the ring.

It was that hoop that gave Dell his first practice into perfecting one of the most efficient and fluid jump shots in the history of NBA – a move that Stephen would later imitate.

After silently watching Dell from behind a curtain in the dining room, Jack would crash towards his son and lecture him on basketball fundamentals. Jack and Dell were another example of a father-and-son tandem chasing an NBA dream.

Dell was playing for the Lakers when a sudden heart attack took his father's life. Dell went back to Virginia not to play at his old hoop but to mourn his father's devastating death.

Years later, Jack's wooden hoop came alive again. The family heard the familiar sound of a ball banging against the backboard and tapping the rim. It was Stephen, who had grown into a puny young boy, trying his grandpa's wooden hoop. Steph not only inherited his grandpa's name but also his old, wooden basketball ring and his undeniable love for sports. "The lessons and love on that old hoop has been passed down to me," Steph says.

However, Steph's shooting skills were still far from exemplary at the time. They were inefficient and easily blocked, a frustration that made Stephen hate shooting at times. Nevertheless, Stephen's spirit was obviously on fire even at a young age. He took a thousand shots every day, practicing under his grandpa's wooden hoop while dripping sweat and tears.

THE BEGINNING OF A DREAM

Stephen spent his younger days in a lush mansion in Charlotte, getting to do whatever he wanted. So he is far from other players' rags-to-riches stories; he grew up with a silver spoon.

However, his parents made sure that his comfort over material things would not pull his character down. Stephen had all the reasons to think that he was the best, yet he remained kind and humble. He did not show even a sign of being a spoiled brat. Sonya, as the homemaker, made sure that Stephen was raised with good traits and strong faith. One way she did so was by letting Stephen do the chores.

The Curry family has always been close with each other. As a grade schooler, Stephen went to Christian Montessori School where his mother was the founder and principal, his aunt his teacher, and his grandmother the cook.

Stephen's parents did not forget to incorporate

Christian values into their daily living. As a family, they would gather every Sunday to participate in church. Meanwhile, Stephen and his siblings would also attend youth Bible studies every Wednesday.

"I can honestly say that my parents were the best. My siblings and I were blessed for having them; they are such great influences in our lives," Steph says about how his parents raised him and his siblings.

These moral foundations have greatly shaped Stephen's unstoppable character. Despite not the best kid in basketball, Steph put on patience as his most important gear. He knew that practicing was the only way he could master his skills. He did not let fear consume the fighter in him. His faith helped him gain confidence. "I believe in myself because I believe in God," Steph says.

Despite being nomads due to Dell's constant change of teams, Stephen still had a memorable childhood. Stephen's early childhood is colored by one-on-one practice games with his brother, Seth, who is only two years younger. Oftentimes, they would play against each other in their backyard basketball court. The boys were only allowed to tag along with their father's games and practices every weekend. Their weekdays were spent at school, home or church. Sonya wanted her sons to understand that basketball was not the only path in life.

When their mother allowed them to tag along with their dad to his NBA games, Steph and Seth wouldn't watch the game. Rather, they would play against each other in the Hornet's practice area while everything and everyone else was getting intense on the main court.

This was always the brothers' routine even when their father transferred to the Raptors. Steph and Seth would sometimes play with the professionals during warm-up. They would even sneak up to the locker area, leading the players to call them gym rats.

Other times, Steph and Seth would look around for pick-up games together with their cousin, Wade. Though the brothers would often get recognized as the sons of a well-known NBA baller, the other boys still looked at them as nothing.

But soon enough, Stephen would turn these doubters into believers, shaking his opponents' calm and enraging them with his incredible shot-making skills. The Curry brothers, being skinny in physical appearance, were easily mocked by the other kids and sometimes drawn into physical fights. Wade, who was larger than most of the boys, would come to the rescue and act as a mediator.

Now, as another Curry in a No. 30 jersey, Stephen pays tribute to his father for making him the player he is today, his dream of becoming a professional basketball player being rooted in his father's influence. Just like any other young boy who considers his father a hero, Stephen just wanted to become like his dad.

And Dell is incredibly proud of his MVP son. He brushes off the praises – either from Stephen or from other people – saying that his son could even outshine his own milestones.

CHAPTER 3
TEENAGE YEARS

HIGH SCHOOL CAREER OF THE PUNY BALLER

When the family moved to Canada as part of Dell's stint with the Raptors, Steph was enrolled in the nearby Queensway Christian College. Draped in a loose jersey that emphasized his small frame, seventh-grader Stephen Curry tried to make his mark.

James Lackey, Queensway's basketball coach, had a good initial impression of Steph's abilities despite his tiny appearance. On their first practice, Lackey asked all the players to warm-up on their own. Stephen immediately stood-up and gave everyone a show. His warm-up was a combination of impressive footwork, net-splashing jumpers, crossovers, and shots.

Anecdotes describe the young baller as akin to a toddler dressed in a long gown for Halloween. His jersey almost exposed his entire chest, his tiny arms flexing with every shot. Yet, despite the lack in build, Stephen Curry played better than most other regular high schoolers. He already had long-ranging shots, impressive dribbling abilities, and a mastery of the game. He was brilliant at manipulating angles and changing directions. He even knew how to use his weakness to his advantage, maximizing his short-area quickness.

The Queensway College was suddenly raving as they began to win with 40 to 50 points in a game – and Curry was carrying the torch.

Legends of Curry's heroic basketball feats have been widely narrated. One of the earliest was when Lackey's team was down by six points at a season-ender. Lackey knew that it would take four or five trips down the court before his players could rack up that many points, and they didn't have kind of time. Lackey's coaching bottle was empty at that moment and he couldn't think of any ideas to even the score.

He called a time-out, not to direct Steph and his teammates, but to prepare them for a possible loss. He had accepted the nearing defeat and wanted his team to do the same. However, Lackey still had one remaining ace, though he didn't know it. He was surprised when Steph spoke up, usually the boy would just listen to his coach and do what he was instructed.

But Steph's fire was ignited. "We are not losing this game. Give me the ball," Stephen said with determination. A few moments later, Steph made two quick three-pointers that changed the game, soon leading Queensway to a 6-point win. Everyone in the crowd saw Stephen Curry's alter-ego, the Baby-faced Assassin, born that day – when the kindest-looking kid on the court turned into a hungry predator.

As Dell's retirement came in 2002, the Curry family decided to move back to the place they considered home – Charlotte. Stephen had to transfer to a nearby school, the Charlotte Christian School where he played basketball for the middle school team. He led the team to three state playoffs and three conference titles. Steph later joined summer camps where he diligently worked to grow and hone his skills.

Even at this young age, Stephen's work ethic was noticed. Charlotte's coach, Shonn Brown, testifies that Stephen had an extraordinary focus and passion. Their practice sessions began at exactly six in the morning. While other kids were still dragging themselves from the bed, Stephen was always the first to show up and the last to leave; displaying the work ethic of a professional player. He would always ask for a recording of the practice and watch it at home to study his moves; preparing for his future opponents.

REJECTIONS AND DOUBT

"Crucial" is an inadequate word to describe the value a collegiate offer has to any aspiring professional baller. Anyone whose life and dreams revolve around basketball knows how essential a university offer can be to a budding career. A college program can hone a player's overall performance and produce a superstar out of him. More importantly, college recruiting letters can create hype for a player, making him a possible top choice for the NBA draft.

Michael Jordan, for example, was a pie that everyone wanted to have at least a bite of. Numerous offers from big universities gave him a big name even before he entered the NBA.

On the other hand, Stephen Curry had no one knocking on his door. As a kid, Curry would often daydream about following his dad's footsteps, and as a part of that dream, Stephen wanted to play for Virginia Tech – just like his father. But, despite being the son of Dell Curry, the man who led Virginia Tech to numerous wins in the past, a walk-on spot was the only thing they would offer Steph, which left what Steph called "a sore spot."

He did not receive offers from other major division schools either. Coming out of high school, Stephen was only 6 feet in height and still not filled out, probably preventing big schools from recruiting him.

He was gifted, they admitted, but he was not strong enough to become a superstar. Most of them only saw what they thought Steph lacked, without examining what else he could bring to the table.

This rejection may have made Stephen upset but he did not let it crush his spirit. Stephen has a fire that blazes up during tough times – a fire that gives him more determination and a refusal to be defeated.

A MATCH MADE IN HEAVEN

Though the winning traits hiding behind Curry's small frame were invisible to most coaches, Davidson College head coach, Bob McKillop, had eyes for them.

The Davidson Wildcats had borne a reputation as a no-hope team since 1969 – in fact, they still have no championship trophy to their name. But Stephen Curry chose them as his college. According to Steph, he liked the plans they had for him. More importantly, Stephen wanted to work with a man of faith, which McKillop was.

Stephen Curry did not disappoint McKillop. His first college game was against Eastern Michigan where he contributed 15 points and 13 turnovers to his team. He immediately upped his performance when he gave 32 points, 9 rebounds and 4 assists in the second game.

With a whopping average of 21.5 points per season, Stephen Curry became the leading player in the Eastern Conference and the second-to-top scorer amongst all freshmen.

In what seemed like a miracle turnaround, the Wildcats began scoring far beyond their wildest imaginations, winning a Southern Conference Season Title with a 29-5 overall record.

Credited for that win, Stephen Curry made a new record for a freshman by scoring his 113th three-point score during the final quarter.

He made another record when he scored his 502nd point in a battle against Chattanooga and made 30 points in an NCAA play-off against Maryland.

Stephen's first season ended sweetly as he was hailed as the Southern Conference Tournament MVP and Freshman of the Year.

However, perhaps his biggest achievement was playing on TEAM USA for the 2007 FIBA U19 World Championships, where he and his teammates brought home a silver medal.

One step at a time, Stephen Curry gathered a legion of local and national believers. During his sophomore year, he began appearing on the national stage, slowly becoming the golden boy of basketball. At the end of his college career, Steph held the record for most three-pointers made in a season.

Steph's game grew more rapidly than his body. He had a hunger for becoming better and better, and contributing something new to the court each year. He was a thinking player, analyzing every score. Steph's father often reminded him to develop powerful movement to make up for his weaknesses, and to find ways to make the shot despite his lack in height.

People who worked close to Curry in college saw his burning passion and discipline. Coach McKillop says that Steph had a vision that allowed him to not only dream of the future but see what was in front of him and make the most out of it.

The Davidson College and Stephen Curry partnership was a match made in heaven, providing for each other's needs and filling in for each other's weaknesses. They both took a chance with each other, an investment that led both of them to glory.

CHAPTER 4
MAKING THE DREAM COME TRUE

THE LUCKY SEVENTH

"Surreal moment" is how Stephen Curry describes the day in 2009 when he was sitting in a green room with his family and heard his name called as the NBA's number 7 draft pick.

Stephen bowed his head in gratitude, thanking God for the opportunity to fulfill a dream as big as getting into the NBA.

Warriors Coach Don Nelson describes their pick of Stephen as a gift. Before the draft night, there were rumors that the New York Knicks were going to use their 8th pick for Curry. So the Golden State Warriors chose him as their 7th pick.

Despite his surprise, Stephen knew that

everything was going according to God's plan. His faith gave him an upbeat attitude; a kind of confidence that trusts life's goodness no matter what happens.

Just like almost every novice player, Curry had doubters who constantly threw criticism at him. But Curry had a winning attitude; he knew how to choose his battles. Dealing with such people would have been a waste of time.

Despite the challenges ahead – a new environment and new people – Curry entered the league with an open mind, determination, and readiness to work hard.

ACCOLADES

Stephen continued his winning streak into his NBA career. The small boy that was once perceived as a weakling managed to rise to the top and make history.

Under the auspices of the Golden State Warriors, Stephen Curry is the franchise leader for the most three-point field goals made in a game, and most three-point field goals over all.

In 2011, Stephen Curry won the NBA Skills Challenge and was the leader for free-throw percentage in the NBA (a title he won in 2015, as well). He also holds the record for the top three-point field goals for the NBA in 2013 and 2014.

In 2015, he was hailed as the Best NBA Player and Best Male Athlete by the ESPY,Awards and awarded BET Sportsman of the Year.

Steph's sacrifices as a team leader were recognized when he was given the NBA

Sportsmanship Award in 2011. He was a grand slam awardee of the Teen Choice Awards for Male Athletes in 2015, recognizing his impact on the youth. As a humanitarian, Stephen is the recipient of the Jefferson Award for Public Service.

In 2018, the Golden State Warriors garnered another NBA Championship under his leadership.

Comment [SC]: What year?

Comment [SC]: What year?

During his years in the NBA, Stephen Curry has displayed a wide variety of extraordinary shots, moves, and strategies on the court that have been documented and widely viewed on social media.

His long list of accolades leads sports analysts to call him a prodigy that only comes once in a blue moon. Stephen Curry is a legend on his own – a rare gem with an extraordinary talent. More than a decade after his first major professional rejection, Stephen is still not the strongest and biggest; yet he has become something else – something more important. He is now the world's best offensive player.

It is not something that he gained overnight, though. Everything he's gained is a product of hard work – 40 minutes of practice every night, a daily 10,000 shots in a gym, and constant study of the NBA's ropes.

BATTLING WITH INJURIES AND DEALING WITH LOSSES

Stephen Curry's life as a baller is filled with bumps and trials that tested his emotional strength. However, he also had his share of physical pain. Those who work in the league know that an injury can not only affect a player's performance, but also end his career.

In Curry's third NBA season, the deciding year for whether his contract would be extended or not, Stephen Curry had injuries that almost took him out of the game completely.

A series of ankle sprains left him with torn ligaments that required serious medication and many surgeries. In what seemed like the pinnacle of Murphy's Law, the same ankle was sprained again even before it fully recovered from the surgeries.

Despite the physical discomfort, Stephen bravely played in the season-opener. However, his performance was greatly affected by the injury.

Stephen also played in the second game but the sprain prevented him from playing in the third. Stephen was only able to play in about one-third of the total games that season.

During the summer of 2018, Warriors fans once again felt the same worry as Steph battled it out against another sprain just as the play-offs were nearing.

But Stephen is a hard worker, and that work seems to have toughened him. He looks at injuries as just a part of the game – a small discomfort compared to all the sweat and tears he has shed throughout his journey.

Stephen has said that he doesn't worry if his injuries prevent him from attending some games. He believes his team is equipped with skills that will bring them to victory without him. There is humility in this statement; admitting that every win is not about him.

But when the losses do come, Steph takes full responsibility. As the leader of the team, he looks at those defeats analytically, extracting the necessary lessons from them, tweaking the mistakes into something useful for future games. After all, Stephen believes that victory becomes sweeter when sprinkled with a little failure at first. Remember that the Baby-faced Assassin gets on fire a little more when faced with challenges.

Yet, Steph puts on his complete humility gear. He does not get defensive when blamed for his team's failures. He does not act like an alpha male with an enraged ego. He does not come out fighting for his honor.

In a loss against Houston in January 2018, for example, Curry said, "I just watched the film and I admit there were two decisions that I did wrong. I had a bad vision on the floor that night. The loss was pretty bad to me and I take responsibility."

CHAPTER 5   MARRIED LIFE

MEETING THE GIRL OF HIS DREAMS

They say that basketball couples are often cursed. More often than not, fame and money peppered with the blinding spotlight can lead a baller and his wife into a tragic separation. Stephen and wife, Ayesha, have successfully broken this curse.

The two were teenage friends who first met through a youth group at their church in Charlotte. Despite Ayesha's beauty and Steph's handsomeness, love at first sight was not their story. Ayesha says that almost all the girls in their church were crushing on Steph, except her. She did not even know that Stephen was a well-known baller in the sports world. Just before they met, Steph had led his team to the Elite 8 in the March Madness Tournament. However, Ayesha seemed unaware of this. In a sea of girls trying to get Steph's attention, there was Ayesha, unassumingly quiet and almost unaware of his presence.

Steph found Ayesha's reaction to his fame refreshing. It convinced him to ask her out on a date. She refused. After all, during one of Ayesha's theater class activities when she was asked to describe her dream partner, she wrote, "No athletes because they are arrogant." Besides, she was not allowed to date in high school. Looking back on this time, Ayesha smiles at how she and Steph were so focused on God during that period.

Eventually, Ayesha moved to Los Angeles to pursue an acting career, and Steph kept his hands busy dribbling and shooting balls in his college games.

Fate finally had its way when Steph was sent to Los Angeles for an ESPY Tournament. Stephen decided to search for her on a social media platform hoping to reconnect.

On his second ask, Ayesha said yes to a date with the budding superstar. Their first date was, as Ayesha puts it, cheesy and romantic. They spent the day on Hollywood Boulevard. Steph exerted all his efforts to impress Ayesha, spending all his pocketmoney for the date. They took souvenir shots with Hollywood impersonators and drank chai tea lattes. Ayesha's negative impressions about Steph started to fade. She began to realize that the guy everyone was crushing on was actually fun to be with.

Months after their first date, while watching a movie with their families over Christmas, Steph finally said, "I love you," to Ayesha. She knew he meant it.

A few years later, in a setting akin to romantic films and novels, Stephen proposed to Ayesha in the same spot where they had their first kiss – the driveway of Ayesha's parent's house in Charlotte . . . in the rain. He had hoped to keep the moment private, but their families were peeking through the window and recording everything.

In 2011, Ayesha and Steph got married at the ages of 22 and 23 respectively. Stephen saw no problem in marrying young. Stephen has said that people should not waste time once they find the right person.

Keeping to their Christian devotions, the couple did not ask for wedding gifts. Rather, they requested their guests to donate to a charity that supports the education of children whose parents are in the armed forces.

Soon after, the couple welcomed their first daughter, Riley, who was born in 2012 – a borderline honeymoon baby.

Steph knew that Ayesha was the woman he wanted to spend the rest of his life with. He knew her deeply – her faith, her aspirations and all her other stories. Perhaps, Stephen is a true romantic – evident in the way he constantly professes his love for Ayesha on his social media posts.

KEEPING THEIR VOWS

Stephen Curry is a family man, giving importance to his wife, children, parents and siblings. This trait is evident in how he lets his family join in his activities on and off the court. It is also reflected through his social media posts, which are mostly photos and videos of him and his family cooking together, dancing and singing.

It is understandable if others may think that the life of someone as big as Stephen Curry should be too hard to handle. His plate is always full – practice sessions, games, endorsements, campaigns, interviews, and other advocacies. Yet, despite the shower of activities, Stephen has remained true to his promise to Ayesha to keep their marriage a top priority.

Steph makes sure to inject a weekly date night into his tight schedule. Steph admits that there are times when he or Ayesha gets distracted with their busy lives. Time for each other – without kids or any other distractions – is an essential ingredient that keeps their marriage happy and healthy, even if they only get away for an hour or two. The date nights are their time to catch up with each other and talk about life.

The couple believes in living in the moment and having fun. On the couple's body are matching tattoos that signify this belief. The tattoos are two arrows pointing to each other; which signify that the past is behind them and the future is ahead, so they live with each other in the moment.

The couple has a pre-game ritual of kissing each other's tattoos. For Ayesha, it is her way of reminding her husband to have fun.

Since his action on the court prevents him from wearing his wedding band, Steph had a wedding band tattooed on his ring finger instead, bearing his wife's first initial. Being the hardcourt crush of many women, the wedding-band tattoo gives him a way to signify his faithfulness to his wife.

Stephen has only appreciative words for his wife. He praises Ayesha for juggling both of their careers and yet being hands-on for the most important people in their lives – their children. He constantly gives credit to his wife for keeping their family close-knit, and doing it with grace.

To make time for each other regardless of what is going on around them is the couple's most important promise. To always be there for each other, to always act as each other's constant support, to encourage each other's happiness and to keep their family as a bonded unit are their top priorities. Stephen Curry, being a family man in every sense of the word, knows how to work these things out.

LIFE AS A DAD

When asked about his biggest fear as a parent, Steph says it is being caught by surprise that his children have grown too fast without him knowing it – without him being there for them every step of the way.

His dream for his children is for them to have a wholesome childhood – away from negative influences – especially since their oldest, Riley, has been approached for advertisements and endorsements.

While other parents would take advantage of this kind of opportunity, Stephen always thinks twice. His fatherhood philosophies revolve around protecting the welfare of his children in every possible way, and media exposure can steal childhood away from them.

Stephen's first daughter, Riley, was born on July 19, 2012. His second daughter, Ryan Carson, was born on July 10, 2015. And on July 2, 2018, the

Currys became a family of five as they welcomed their baby boy, Canon.

To Stephen, his children are his biggest encouragement, giving him reasons to play more and play better. "Kids put life into perspective," he says. Since becoming a father, no matter how his day goes, whether he scores well or not, he does not seem to care. What matters to him is the fact that his children's lovely smiles are going to greet him when he comes home. "When I see my children's faces happy to see me, that makes everything all right," Steph shares.

The way his children impact his life goes far beyond what Steph can put into words. For him, his children give him reasons to live.

This is why Stephen lost his calm when he heard comments that bringing his kids into his activities is inappropriate.

After the Championship game in 2015, Steph, as MVP, had to grant a press conference appearance. In the middle of his interview, Riley, who was sitting in his lap, took over the spotlight. At one point, Riley commanded her father to shut up and then sang into the microphone.

Stephen received mixed comments over this incident. While some saw a sweet father, others were not pleased. However, Stephen knows what battles are worth fighting. And for him, listening to comments about his parenting style is not worth his time.

Steph knows that there will never be a perfect parenting style – not even his. He admits that he makes mistakes sometimes. When it comes to parenting, he believes that there are really no rules to follow, he acts based on his instinct – on what he feels is right for his kids. He does not let anyone dictate his decisions about his children's welfare and protection.

When it comes to letting his family tag along to his activities, Steph will always remain unapologetic. He says that it is simply one of his ways to have bonding time with them. The demand of his work to move from place to place is what Steph considers the most challenging part of fatherhood. There are times when guilt creeps into Stephen's heart knowing that his children are growing fast; they are changing every day and he is missing quite a lot.

As much as possible, the loving father wants to be involved in his children's lives. So Steph is thankful for the help technology offers. He makes sure that his children see his face every day, even if he is away for a stretch of time so he can engage them in conversation. He asks questions and shows interest in their lives. Stephen knows that the time he spends with them and the technology he uses is limited, but he wants to make his children feel that he is close to them even if he is far away.

Stephen is a kind of father who is not afraid of showing off his affection for his children. "He is not too cool for school," Ayesha says in appreciation of her husband's parenting style.

At home, Stephen is not a superstar but simply a loving husband and father. He goes down and dirty on the floor to play with his daughters over dolls and princesses. The sweetest thing of all is perhaps the fact that he never runs out of patience with his kids; something that Ayesha admittedly lacks. Therefore, for Ayesha and Steph, theirs is a kind of a balanced co-parenting act.

CHAPTER 6

OFF-THE-COURT ADVOCACIES

INSPIRING THE YOUTH

Stephen Curry is the face of the present generation of basketball and he is an agent of inspiration to future players.

As part of an initiative to promote sportsmanship in youth across the globe, he hosts youth clinics whenever and wherever he can. Recently, he also started an online basketball training program which is divided into two major parts with 17 lessons in total; each one ranges from 15-20 minutes.

The first part of the program features the superstar-coach in a gym giving active instructions on proper technique in balance, shooting, dribbling and other movements. Each lesson comes with a couple of drills that help hone the student's proper form.

In the second part of Steph's classes, he shows how to be a thinker on the court, going over game clips and discussing his thoughts on proper decision-making, harnessing the fundamentals discussed in the first part of the class.

Stephen Curry says that being able to influence fans across the globe is special for him. He has a blazing passion for basketball and wants everyone to feel the kind of bliss that he breathes in when playing.

In his clinic sessions, Stephen doesn't only teach basketball fundamentals, he imparts lessons about important values and virtues on and off the court, with deep emphasis on being a real team player.

Stephen believes that form and mechanics must work together. Taking a cue from his father's game mentality, Steph believes that player development must start at an early age, beginning with training the physical body, then mastering basketball fundamentals and the spirit of determination.

HUMANITARIAN ACTS

The media calls Stephen's impact on the public the "Steph Effect." Stephen has built his reputation and credibility over his years in the NBA, becoming an influence not just on basketball but in other causes and advocacies as well. Instead of creating noise about his own name, Stephen Curry focuses his time and effort on philanthropies.

Since 2012, Stephen Curry has been working with the 'Nothing but Nets' campaign of the United Nations to help protect families in Africa from malaria. He also sponsors shoe donation drives for African children.

Curry is also an active partner of United Playaz, an organization that focuses on youth development and violence prevention.

Curry has a soft spot for the youth and he values education. From his college days to his early days in the NBA, Steph helped a youth education center by being a reading tutor. With his wider influence, he has started raising donations for the center by hosting golf tournaments.

Since 2010, he has used a similar strategy to raise donations to help military families send their children to school. He also donated a portion of his 2015 and 2016 MVP winnings to the cause.

Stephen has worked together with former president Barack Obama to provide financial support and mentorship to the youth through programs called "My Brother's Keeper" and "Brotherhood Crusade."

Curry shares his blessings by donating parts of his own earnings as well. He donated to NFL quarterback Colin Kaepernick's million-dollar pledge.

People who work close with Curry in his philanthropic campaigns admire how he exudes integrity and composure when using his platform to stand up for what is right.

"All the noise that is going around the world, especially in the country [United States of America] actually put things in perspective. It simply implies that we are all small in the world but nevertheless, we can still do something good and find our own small ways to leave an impact." Steph says.

Steph's humanitarian activities started during his younger days when his father was still playing on the courts of the NBA. Steph, together with his siblings, would volunteer in several local organizations in Charlotte.

Unlike other influencers who simply raise awareness through superficial campaigns, Stephen works through personal interactions. He visits refugees, listens to mothers, plays with children, and interacts with the sick. It is admirable how Steph does it all with such humility, respect and dignity.

People whose lives were touched by Stephen clearly remember how the superstar approached them with care and thoughtfulness – how Steph interacted with them human-to-human. He has ears that are eager to listen to other people's stories and a heart that never runs out of space for understanding.

"You can always have a glimpse of people's stories through pictures but when I get to be there for them, first-hand, it just validates my mission," Stephen says.

GROWING ENDORSEMENTS AND CAMPAIGNS

His growing accolades, charming aura, and established credibility have made Stephen Curry a bankable celebrity endorser. As the media describes it, Steph puts a halo over the brand he is endorsing. While other celebrities simply accept what is offered to them without hesitation, Steph makes sure to only accept endorsements and campaigns that leave a purely positive impact on the public.

His partnership with Under Armour, for example, features sneakers that have Morse code on the soles that, once decoded, reveal a Bible verse. Other sneakers have the phrase "I can do all things" inscribed on the tongue as reference to Philippians 4:13 in the Bible.

In his endorsements for a particular brand of phone, his aim is to raise the message of believing in one's self despite the distracting words of doubts thrown by others.

There are still numerous endorsement deals under his name including a brand of deodorant, car, water filtration pitcher, group chat application, and bank.

Endorsement offers come to Stephen on a daily basis, but Steph only agrees to endorse products and services that reflect his advocacies and personality. "I only accept ones that feel true to me and leave a clean message," Stephen says.

CHAPTER 7
PHILOSOPHIES AND BELIEFS

A DEVOUT CHRISTIAN

Stephen Curry pounds his chest and points to the sky – a pre-game gesture he has performed since the beginning of his career. The ritual, which he developed with his mom, is Steph's simple way of reminding himself that he represents and has a heart for God.

Steph is never shy about expressing his faith. He prays for his co-players and coaches before a game. He prays for other people who he thinks need his support. He writes pieces narrating his testimony. Together with his wife and children, he worships God through church services. He and Ayesha record these church services and broadcast them over live platforms.

69

Stephen Curry is known as a man of faith. It is evident in the words he speaks and the actions he performs on and off the court. Since the first time he amazed the public with his shot-making skills, Stephen Curry has been consistently giving all the credit to God. He loudly praises Him for all that he has accomplished.

In every speech he delivers, like his acceptance speech for his MVP Award, Stephen is very vocal about his relationship with God. He simply considers himself a humble servant of the Lord. "I can't find the words to adequately say how important my faith is to how I play and who I am," Stephen said when he won his first MVP Award.

In a written testimony, Stephen shares when and how he accepted God into his life. According to this piece, his childhood was filled with the presence of God.

As a fourth-grader, Stephen heard the gospel, walked into the aisle and vowed to accept the

Lord in his life and to spend all his days glorifying Him. After that, his parents, ensuring that Steph's vow was clear to him, continued to teach him about the faith.

Growing up in a Christian school, Steph was blessed to hear the gospel every day. It helped him secure a relationship with God that is built in trust and confidence. Even during the time when his childhood dream of playing for Virginia Tech was not granted, his heart was still full of gratitude. Despite a lack of interest from all the other schools, Steph was still hopeful, feeling that it was all just part of God's bigger plans. He surrendered everything to the Lord. With trust and confidence, he believed that what God had orchestrated was far bigger than what he asked for.

The Warrior believes that God has been too good to him. In return, he promises to always give his best in whatever he does, especially basketball. He sees basketball as a way of glorifying God, and giving back all the blessings and strength that He has bestowed upon him. He uses basketball to lead more people towards God.

He believes that at the end of the day, he already has a place in heaven – and that spot is a blessing that no other earthly prize or trophy could ever replace. God may have given him the talent to play basketball for a living, yet he knows that it is just a game that can be taken from him at any moment. Therefore, his faith pushes him to continue getting better every day.

"There is more to me beyond the jersey that I wear all the time, and that is God breathing and living inside of me," Stephen testifies.

DISCIPLINE AND A HUNGER FOR EXCELLENCE

Stephen, as a loving son, consistently honors his parents and praises them for instilling discipline in his upbringing. His family has been a key element in Curry's growth as an athlete. They were his support system and gravitational pull that reminded him to embrace humility.

In his MVP acceptance speech, Stephen Curry told the audience that without his parents' constant guidance and discipline, he would not have become the player that he is today.

There was even a time when his mother, Sonya, prevented him from joining his first-season game in high school because he forgot to do the chores. As the MVP, Curry smiled while looking back at the day he told his teammates that he wouldn't be able to play because he didn't wash the dishes. It was embarrassing then but he sees it now as a good foundation for building his character.

This kind of discipline goes hand-in-hand with his desire to excel. Behind Stephen Curry's boy-next-door smile on the court is a blazing competitiveness. Coach McKillop shares that Steph has a hunger for excellence. "His quest for excellence is like a fire that is raging within him," McKillop says.

But Steph's competitiveness is balanced with confidence. Steph does not care if he misses a couple of shots because he knows that he is going to make many future shots.

Winning is his goal in every game. Having titles like the star, the captain, and the likes mean nothing to him if they do not involve winning. The failure to win just makes these titles meaningless.

HUMILITY AND SELFLESSNESS

When Coach Brown asked the young Curry to take more shots, he initially refused, saying he didn't want his teammates to think that he was selfish. So Brown explained that Steph must take more shots if he wanted the team to win. Curry got it – he needed to step up.

As early as his student-athlete days, Curry's selflessness has been evident. He knows that as a team captain, the game is not about him. His role is to set his people up to score. He has become a beautiful contradiction: the prototype of a giver-shooter. He is confident yet humble – a magical combination that only he seems to possess.

Curry has become a superstar, and his status rightfully comes with a perk of entitlement. However, his success has not yet exploded his ego.

Curry gives the credit for his humility to his parents, who instilled selflessness in him like it was just a form of breathing.

When he received his MVP Award in 2015, Stephen's speech included thanking specific people – especially his teammates – one-by-one. He mentioned every single player on his team to let them know of their importance to his game. Whenever his team wins under his leadership, he does not take all the credit. He never did.

Stephen Curry possesses the most winning trait of all – humility and selflessness. He knows how much he can contribute to the team, yet he steps down when needed to let others shine. He opens up space for his teammates; making room for them to take shots. It may look unwise to some but for Stephen Curry, that is just what a captain must do – build an empire through sacrifice.

For his teammates, Stephen's lack of entitlement is contagious. For a long time, money has been quite a big issue in the NBA. However, the Warriors keep quiet and shy away from this bait. Why would they fall for it, when their greatest player is receiving just enough money and yet is still happy and content?

Stephen's humility is also evident in how he never forgets his roots – the people who made him who he is today. In fact, Stephen and his coaches in middle school and college are still in touch today. At times, Stephen visits his hometown, especially the Charlotte Christian School, in summers. The letters TCC, which stands for Charlotte's "trust, commitment, care" motto, are tattooed in his body; reminding him of his humble beginnings.

Indeed, Stephen is a rare breed of superstar. He shuns the entitlement that comes with his status and chooses the simple route instead.

CHAPTER 8
BEYOND THE LIMELIGHT

FROM THE PERSPECTIVE OF FRIENDS AND COLLEAGUES

Stephen Curry's impact on the fans, youth and the public is undeniable. However, it isalso true that he also inspires his colleagues – even players who have already made a name for themselves.

Kobe Bryant, for example, points to Stephen Curry as a source of inspiration. According to Jordan Clarkson, Kobe once instructed him to study Stephen's moves and take inspiration from them. Kobe emphasized that everyone must take note of how Stephen moves without the ball.

Los Angeles Lakers Coach Byron Scott also uses Stephen Curry's name when giving his team some basketball lessons. He instructs them to look up to Steph and learn from him. "Just by watching Stephen play on the court, he can already give you an idea of how much work he puts in. We must give him credit for being a team-player, he handles his teammates well and everyone loves playing with him because he is unselfish," Scott says.

Stephen Curry is a role model to his colleagues like Larry Nance, Jr. of the Lakers. Just like Steph, Larry also went to a smaller school in college. As he watched Steph rise from his humble beginnings, Larry got encouragement to follow in his footsteps.

Orlando Magic's Victor Oladipo says that he tries to carry on Stephen's legacy by getting better each year.

Stephen Curry, on the other hand, admits taking inspiration from NBA legends like Michael Jordan and Kobe Bryant. He admires how the two players used their influence to inspire the youth, especially in the field of sports. He hopes to pass on that same kind of legacy – giving inspiration to the younger generation. He looks forward to the future and hopes that twenty years from now, he will hear beautiful stories from kids who grew up watching him play.

SPENDING HIS FREE TIME

Stephen Curry's passion for basketball is as bright as the sun. It is crystal clear. But Stephen is also into other sports, like golf. He is, in fact, NBA's greatest golfer.

Stephen's love for golf started when he was just 6; playing with his father in what seemed to be just a hobby that eventually turned into love. He was Charlotte High School's best golfer. Recently, *Golf Digest* revealed that Curry took the 14th spot on their "List of Professional Athletes on the Golf Course."

Curry's friendship with former president Barack Obama was strengthened by their time together on the golf course.

Aside from golf, the superstar's other favorite hobby is organizing the garage. This hobby may look odd, especially if done by someone who is known for dazzling the fans on the court. However, Stephen says that it is what gets him in the zone. The garage is his arena at home. He finds comfort in re-arranging the equipment, organizing the shoe boxes, and cleaning the shelves.

Off the court, he never acts like a superstar but simply a human. As Ayesha puts it, "He never calls himself a basketball player. He is simply a man positioned by God to do something good, which is basketball."

Stephen is also often in the kitchen together with his family; either helping with the cooking or simply enjoying Ayesha's prepared meals. The Curry's kitchen has always been busy given Ayesha's life as a homemaker, cookbook author and restaurateur.

LOOKING INTO THE FUTURE

As further proof of his versatility, Stephen Curry is about to conquer the world of media production. He has recently started his own production company called Unanimous Media. Stephen aims to produce programs that focus on family, sports, and faith. Recently, he was able to seal a partnership with Sony to bring his faith and core values to the big screen.

Stephen's production company already has a line-up of possible films to produce including a comedy entitled "Church Hoppers," a play on the film "Wedding Crashers." They also plan to create an animated biblical feature.

While others try to create films based on modern themes, Curry does not mind being called corny for producing biblical features. He produces films as a way of extending his beliefs. "I just want to share what I personally believe in, but it is not about me hitting people with bibles in the head. I just want to inspire as many people as possible,"

Stephen says.

Taking a cue from his own experiences, Stephen has always been fascinated about dreamers and their journeys towards success. As a kick-off to his producing career, he has recently launched his own YouTube series entitled "5 Minutes from Home." The episodes feature Curry interviewing dreamers from different walks of life and getting to know the stories behind their achievements.

The Warriors' 2018 championship battle was a difficult one for Curry. His injuries almost stopped him from playing, and the Warriors did not have home court advantage. But these challenges made winning the championship all the sweeter.

Though Stephen has a bright vision for his team, he knows that each season will require more hard work and diligent planning. To prepare, he plans to focus on training camps and conditioning his body. He sees his body as his biggest investment —allowing him to move, cut, and switch on his defenses. He feeds his hunger for excellence by investing a lot of his time in getting stronger each year. "As my career continues, I want to be durable as possible and find different ways to maintain my body and strength. I am not a type of player who goes above the rim, not the high player type of guy; staying strong is the only way I can keep up with all the games I play," Stephen says.

There is more that Stephen can still offer in the years to come. He never fails to surprise the crowd with his versatility on and off the court. One moment he is making a surprise three-pointer, but the next finds him in the kitchen or the production area. But no matter what endeavor he chooses, his trademark smooth three-pointers and dazzling moves will always be Stephen Curry's legacy.

Stephen surely wants a long-term future with the Golden States Warriors. He loves the team he is playing for and he loves where he is at. The Bay Area is a home to Stephen Curry and his family.

CONCLUSION

Success does not come by accident, and Stephen Curry shows us why. Sometimes, we struggle to keep our faith, especially when trials block our way. Most of the time, we see rejections in a bad light.

However, Stephen Curry shows us how to do it the other way around. His views on rejection – as merely a small part of God's bigger plan – is an inspiring take on life's difficulties.

Success is difficult to achieve only to those who do not believe in their dreams. However, dreams must go hand in hand with actions and determination. As Stephen Curry said, "Greatness is about mastering the process of the game."

That, indeed, is the legacy of Stephen Curry – a winning attitude that cares more about the mastery of the game than the achievement itself.

Made in the USA
Columbia, SC
16 December 2019